For the Love of Alberta

Paul Buller

(2015-10-29)

DEDICATION

Dedicated to all the hard-working, resourceful, compassionate, ethical, family-oriented Albertans who make this province such a great place to live, work, play and raise my family.

CONTENTS

1 BACKGROUND

In 2015 Albertans decided they had enough of the reigning Progressive Conservative (PC) government that had been in power for decades. Of all the parties they could choose from, they elected the New democrat Party (NDP).

The NDP!?!

In Alberta?!?!

The prospect horrified me and I wondered what state of affairs could possibly lead Albertans to lose their collective minds. Albertans, of all people, ought to be intimately aware of the benefits of right-leaning government policies. After all, despite whatever mistakes the PC party had made over the course of its reign, the province of Alberta thrived, grew and prospered in very large part because of right-leaning government policies.

Upon reflection, however, it occurred to me that perhaps there are lots of people who don't know why it is that right-leaning government policies tend to work, and why left-leaning government policies do not, even though the left makes promises that sound both grander and more compassionate than those on the right end of the political spectrum. The promises definitely sound better, but the delivery is woefully inadequate. Because the focus of my attention is on left-leaning policies in general, while I will discuss certain specific NDP policies (as presented in the 2015 election[1]), I will spend most of my time addressing broadly accepted left-leaning policies whether or not the Alberta NDP explicitly endorsed those policies in the 2015 election.

And so, in this mini book, I do my best to offer at least a first-pass explanation of why right-leaning government policies tend to work better than left-leaning. And why it would be in the best interest of Albertans to discharge the NDP of their place in power at the earliest possible opportunity. Or, more correctly, to get rid of left-leaning public policy. If the NDP suddenly reverses course, abandons their left-leaning policies, and embraces right-leaning policies then, by all means, let them stay.

---

[1] At the time of this writing you could download it from the link here - http://www.albertandp.ca/platform

2 DO LEFT-LEANING POLICIES REALLY NOT WORK?

Before we get too far I should provide at least a quick justification for my concern about left-leaning policies. And to do so, I look back to the province of my birth; Manitoba[2]. Since the NDP were first elected into power in that province in 1969 they have held office for 31 of the 46 years from then until the present – nearly 70% of that period. From 1999 until the present they have remained in power without a break. Manitoba is truly a left-leaning province, through and through.

What effect has that had on Manitoba? Well, ask the many ex-Manitobans – like my own family – who have left the province. According to Statistics Canada, every year (for which they have records[3]) more Canadians have moved out of Manitoba than have moved into it. In other

---

[2] https://en.wikipedia.org/wiki/Politics_of_Manitoba

[3] http://www.statcan.gc.ca/pub/91-209-x/2014001/article/14012/tbl/tbl1-eng.htm

words, Manitoba may be a great place to visit, but every year thousands of people decide it is not a preferable place to live.

Can we really blame the NDP for that? Surely other factors are at play, right? Well, let's take a look at Saskatchewan as another example. Like Manitoba, Saskatchewan has endured many years of NDP rule since they were first elected to power in 1971. And also like Manitoba, Canadians have tended to leave Saskatchewan more often than moving into it during that period. Below is a snapshot of the migration trends for the province since 2001; numbers below zero indicate more people leaving than coming.

Year	Migration (Sask)
2001/2002	-8,820
2002/2003	-5,141
2003/2004	-4,521
2004/2005	-9,515
2005/2006	-7,083
2006/2007	1,549
2007/2008	4,171
2008/2009	2,983
2009/2010	2,153
2010/2011	545
2011/2012	1,878

Notice how something happened around 2006 / 2007. Change was in the air, it would seem. Part of that change was the fact that the Saskatchewan Party became the ruling party in 2007. The Saskatchewan Party is a centre-right party[4]. Apparently the people of Saskatchewan were done with left-leaning policies. Even though the centre-right Saskatchewan Party did not run the province until 2007, ever since they first came on the scene in 1999 the NDP have steadily felt the impact of their presence; losing seats and eventually losing power.

And when the NDP were removed from power (today the Saskatchewan Party enjoys a commanding majority government – the NDP have been reduced to single digit seat count) people started moving back to Saskatchewan faster than they moved out of the province. Coincidence? That seems unlikely.

If you live in Alberta I shouldn't have to tell you about migration trends of this province; every Albertan knows about the steady, massive, influx of Canadians into our province. Statistics Canada confirms what Albertans are well aware of; for almost every year on record Canadians have been moving into Alberta far faster than they have been leaving Alberta. And our government? Until recently, steadily right-leaning (since 1971). Coincidence? Again, that seems unlikely.

Of course, countless disclaimers are in order. What inspires people to move into or out of any given province at any given time is surely the result of a very wide range of factors. For instance, I know of several people who built their career in Alberta and retired on the West Coast. That has little or nothing to do with the politics or economics in either province. And, as a friend of mine pointed out when he read a previous version of this book, many other very significant factors were at play in Alberta and Saskatchewan around the same time.

---

[4] https://en.wikipedia.org/wiki/Saskatchewan_Party

It would be unwise to presume we can reduce it all down to the single factor of how right- or left-leaning the government is in a province. But as I will show later there does seem to be a general trend between how "progressive" a province is and how eager people are to get out of it. While the migration patterns of Saskatchewan cannot be entirely laid at the feet of their elected officials, it would be unwise of us to ignore that contributing factor. After all, an entirely left-leaning province (Manitoba) has seen steady departures, an entirely right-leaning province (Alberta) has seen steady arrivals, and the province that has swung between the two political extremes (Saskatchewan) has seen both arrivals and departures. That, and other data I examine later, seems like too much of a trend to be mere coincidence.

So if you don't trust me that left-leaning policies are harmful to a province, just look at the impact the NDP has had on other provinces where they have been in power for an extended period of time. Or, more to the point, ask the many Canadians who have left those provinces during NDP reign.

3 POVERTY

People have written entire books on political theory, so the following chapters will be just a quick snapshot of a few of the "hot button" issues that typically contrast left-leaning and right-leaning political policies. A little more information can be found in the appendices.

The first issue is poverty. This is an issue that left-leaning parties make a rather big deal of, but (and this may surprise you) research shows that left-leaning ideas about how to deal with poverty actually tend to increase and entrench poverty, not alleviate it. This is expertly shown and explained in the book "When Helping Hurts" (Steve Corbett & Brian Fikkert). Another good book on the subject – and a bit of a shorter read – is "Toxic Charity." Neither of these books are aimed at government policy directly, but there is a striking resemblance between what they claim private charities are doing wrong and the platforms left-leaning political parties.

The key point that "When Helping Hurts" makes is that poverty is not, fundamentally, about a lack of money. Lack of money is a symptom of the problem, but it is not the root of the problem. When poor people are asked to describe poverty,

"Poor people typically talk in terms of shame, inferiority, powerlessness, humiliation, fear, hopelessness, depression, social isolation, and voicelessness. North American audiences tend to emphasize a lack of material things such as food, money, clean water, medicine, housing, etc." (page 51)

The fundamental issues of poverty are not, at their root, related to money. As the authors observe, "The problem goes well beyond the material dimension, so the solutions must go beyond the material as well." (page 52)

And the fact that government policies can either create the conditions for poverty, or make it difficult for people to get out of poverty, is briefly touched on in the book as the authors describe some of the history associated with the Federal Housing Administration and the current welfare system in the USA (pages 85-86). When a political party puts poverty front and center in their list of issues that they want to "fix" you can be almost certain they are going to make the problem worse, not better.

And the NDP have a history of focusing on poverty and the "little guy," poor people. For instance, in the 2015 election one of the promises the NDP made was to introduce a new income tax paradigm in Alberta; getting rid of the flat tax of 10% for all income levels. They want the lowest income earners to only pay 10% while the highest income earners pay more. This idea has been widely implemented across Canada, but rather than helping the poor, it is associated with an increase in low-income earners. The policy sounds great on paper, but it would seem that it actually increases poverty!

As I show in Appendix A, those provinces that have the greatest difference between the tax rate for the highest income earners, and the tax rate for the lowest income earners (what I call the "tax spread") also tend to have the highest proportion of low-income earners. Furthermore, the average income for everybody in those provinces with a more "progressive" tax structure tends to be lower too. The data from South of the border doesn't dispute this trend (though it is a little fuzzier). Progressive economic policies are also associated with a lower GDP and less generosity from the citizens with respect to charitable giving. This is especially pronounced with respect to high income earners; as the tax rate on the wealthiest is raised, the charitable giving in the province drops.

A similar correlation exists between higher taxes for corporations (another favorite policy for left-leaning politicians) and low-income earners and median income in the province. The more you tax the large corporations, the greater the number of citizens that end up in low-income situations, and the median income for the province drops. And this doesn't seem to be helped by offering tax breaks to small businesses either.

In fact, taxes of all kinds seem to make things worse, not better. Even provincial sales tax is associated with negative economic results for the province.

But don't trust the numbers, trust Canadians. According to Statistics Canada data (also provided in Appendix A) Canadians are more likely to move away from progressive provinces (higher tax spread, higher minimum wage, etc) and into less progressive provinces. Sometimes when we look at charts and figures we forget that these represent real people, real families. A drop in GDP may look bad on paper, but it looks particularly horrible for the man who loses his job and can no longer support his family. It looks terrible for the little girl pulled out of her school, her community and established friendships because her family is relocating to a less progressive province where the economy is thriving and there are jobs for her parents.

It may seem counter-intuitive, but if you really want to help the low-income earners in your province – if you want to actually take a bite out of poverty instead of just talking about it – keep the tax rate the same across all income levels and keep all taxes (even the corporate tax rate for large corporations) as low as reasonably possible. When we demand that the high-income earners and large corporations pay more in taxes then we actually find that the impact on your average citizen is harmful, not helpful; they have less means to support themselves. "Progressive" tax structures are supposed to help the less fortunate, but ironically they seem to contribute to the problem of poverty instead of alleviating it.

Earlier I mentioned that the book "When Helping Hurts" clarifies that poverty is not, at root, a problem about money. One of the reasons left-leaning policies don't work is because they try to deal with poverty from a financial perspective. The assumption seems to be that if we distribute the money more evenly (i.e. take from the rich and give to the poor) then somehow poverty will be reduced. But research shows that this strategy – trying to solve a non-money problem through monetary means – actually makes the problem worse. The higher the tax spread – i.e. the more progressive the tax structure – the more people seem to get stuck in the low income bracket.

Why? Because poverty is not, at root, a problem about money. Money won't solve it. This was expertly described in "When Helping Hurts" if you would like a deeper explanation of the issue.

So when those on the right-leaning end of the political spectrum do not enthusiastically support some "progressive" proposal for poverty alleviation, hopefully this will help you understand that the lack of support may not be due to a lack of empathy or compassion, but rather it may be inspired by a concern over the lack of results. Right-leaning individuals are so concerned with helping people out of poverty that their first priority is to correct a system that contributes to poverty in the first place. While left-leaning policies sound far more compassionate and concerned with the "little guy" unfortunately they suffer from the law of unintended consequences; they create more of a problem than they solve. They strive to help, but they do more harm than good.

4 FAMILY

In the introduction I clarified that I wanted to address left-leaning and right-leaning policies in general, not always in reference to the NDP platforms in the recent election. Family structures wasn't an issue in this last election. Indeed, family structures hasn't been an election issue in a long time. Even right-leaning folks who typically stand for a fairly traditional understanding of family have more or less been silenced on this issue due to immense social pressure. Even if most right-leaning folks dare not stick their necks out on the issue, we typically hold the traditional family unit as being of paramount importance.

Why is family so important? Well, let's start at the end goal and work our way back from there.

For a society to flourish, the individuals within a society need to flourish; they need to be healthy. If the individuals within a society are generally healthy (not just physically, but emotionally, psychologically, etc) then society as a whole has a much better shot at being healthy too. It is pretty hard to imagine a healthy society comprised of generally unhealthy individuals!

One of the most significant factors that influences the health of an adult is their childhood. The better a person's childhood the more likely that person will be to grow up into a well-rounded, healthy adult. The Spring 2015[5] issue of "Apple Magazine" (a publication from Alberta Health Services) had a number of articles touching on various aspects of child brain development and some of the unfortunate side effects that arise if brain development does not follow its proper course. In the article, "We see addictions differently" (page 68-69) the author describes some of the various possible roots of addictions, "early childhood and brain development, adverse childhood experiences, epigenetics … and even personality."

In an article entitled, "Passing a new judgement" (page 73 – 76) the author describes how the legal system is becoming increasingly aware of the brain development aspects of some criminal activity. For instance, "The human condition – mental illness, homelessness, addictions, violence, family breakup – plays out daily in Alberta's courts." Related to the previously cited article on addiction, this article describes how "addiction is a brain disease that is more likely to affect people who have had three or more adverse childhood experiences."

So important is childhood development to adult health that, in the introduction to that issue of the magazine, the editor of the magazine observes,

"Healthy childhood development … is the foundation for educational achievement, economic productivity, responsible citizenship and lifelong health, leading ultimately to successful parenting of the next generation, strong communities and a healthy economy." (page 9)

Wow; it would seem a lot is at stake in one's childhood.

---

[5] http://www.applemag-digital.com/applemag/spring_2015#pg1

But the magazine makes a point of teaching us that healthy brain development can be seriously hindered by "adverse childhood experiences" (ACEs) as the magazine states in a number of places. What, exactly, does that phrase mean; what is an "adverse childhood experience?" Fortunately that issue of the magazine has an entire article on exactly that subject, entitled, "When ACEs are too high." (page 43 – 44). One of the many ACEs described is when, "a child's parents separate or divorce."

In fact, divorce is such a significant ACE that the magazine devotes an entire article to that one ACE alone. The article – entitled, "Avoiding the breakup earthquake of divorce" – offers suggestions for how to minimize the impact of divorce on kids. However, the article carefully avoids claiming that the negative effects of divorce can be completely eliminated; divorce is one "adverse childhood experience" that will always leave a scar.

And even if a couple manages to divorce in a civilized manner, that situation is still less-than-ideal. Another article entitled, "Parents are joining an evolution" (page 45 – 46) describes the early stages of brain development in a child and how the brain development is influenced by the child's everyday experiences. The author observes, "this is why relationships with the adults in their lives are so critically important." The article goes on to clarify, "We're beginning to understand that to the extent that dads are positively involved [in child rearing], the children's and the mothers' lives are better." Divorce obviously makes it significantly more difficult for dads to be actively involved in child-rearing, so even the most civilized divorce is inherently harmful to children.

All of these realities lead Michelle Gagnon, the vice president and chief operating officer of Alberta Family Wellness Initiative, to conclude, "Early childhood matters, enormously. We're developing a shared understanding of what early childhood development means to Albertans and the implications related to policy, practice, and research." (Why it takes a Village – page 58-61). The article goes on to observe that "family is the most significant influence in a child's life."

Did you catch that? Let me repeat, "family is the most significant influence in a child's life."

Given the importance of a healthy family for a positive upbringing for children, it should come as no surprise that social conservatives are rather protective of the gold standard family arrangement that is statistically much more likely to produce a positive family environment – biological parents raising their children in a life-long, stable, marriage.

But is marriage really that important? Can't couples that live together in a long-term, committed relationship be just as good of parents?

It is very common for couples in Alberta (and elsewhere) to live together prior to marriage; often instead of marriage. Common-law family arrangements (otherwise referred to as "cohabitation" in the literature) is, unfortunately, just as unhealthy as it is common. There have been many studies on common-law relationships, given their prevalence, and the conclusions of these studies are so consistent that scholars have coined the term "cohabitation effect" to describe the negative effect that cohabitation has on family stability and quality. Couples who cohabit before getting married consistently have lower relationship quality, poorer communication, more conflict and are more likely to divorce if they do get married.

In Appendix B I provide a list of studies and papers relating to the sociology of families; several with a focus on cohabitation. I also take a look at some community and crime statistics within Calgary (my home base) to see if the literature is being "lived out" in our backyards. Indeed it is.

Communities with a higher percentage of traditional "nuclear" families also tend to have lower crime, higher median income, more education and better career success (fewer unemployed people). If the nuclear family is broken, or bypassed altogether as in the case of common-law relationships, crime tends to go up, income drops and unemployment rises.

Does that sound like a good situation for kids? Even if the couple that cohabits prior to marriage ends up getting married prior to having kids, they are still more likely to divorce and we've already seen the impact that has on kids. The data from Calgary shows that communities with a high proportion of separated / divorced people also tend to experience all the same negative effects mentioned above. Not only is divorce more likely in common-law relationships, the literature indicates that other ACEs are also more likely to be present including physical abuse, substance abuse, addictions and so on. Many cohabiting couples make their situation work without all of these negative consequences, but too many of these couples suffer from the "cohabitation effect" to treat that living arrangement as an equal alternative to marriage. Cohabiting is generally not good for the couple, nor for any children that they end up having whether they marry or not.

When social conservatives place biological, married, families front-and-center in their priority list, it is not out of some misguided attempt to hold on to an outdated moral standard from generations past. It's because that arrangement is best for women and children. While social "progressives" would like to broaden the definition of "family" – and approve of an ever-increasing range of sexual lifestyle choices and attitudes – social conservatives realize that these alternatives are not equally effective in creating stable communities and raising healthy kids; our nation's future citizens. Sociology confirms this, time and again. As with poverty, social conservatives tend to have the eye on the actual results. We actually want children everywhere to have a healthy childhood and the opportunity to grow up to be, as the apple magazine describes, "responsible citizens" who enjoy "lifelong health."

While left-leaning policies sound far more compassionate and concerned with the "little guy" unfortunately they suffer from the law of unintended consequences. They strive to help, but they do more harm than good to the littlest guys in our midst; our children. Right-leaning policies work because children are built in such a way that they need both their biological mom and biological dad for their entire lives. We simply want policies that align with reality; in this case realities of what is best for kids.

Let me leave you with one concluding thought. Despite the fact that traditional marriage is so vitally important to society many, oh so many, families have broken this mold. So many couples live common-law. So many people are divorced. There are so many single parents out there. The fact that these situations are difficult on children (and usually the parents too) is not grounds to look down on these folks, or blame them, personally, for societies problems. Instead, our response should be two-fold. First, we should work hard to preserve the ideal situation; traditional families. We should find ways to encourage people who are not yet married, or recently married, to lay the appropriate foundation for success.

On the other hand, we need to work with those who find themselves in one of the less-than-ideal situations to make the best of their circumstances. Knowing that these family situations puts their children at a disadvantage, how can we help them regain the lost ground? Rather than a pointed finger, let's extend a helping hand.

5 ECONOMICS

In the 2015 election the NDP made a few promises that sounded both responsible and compassionate. As with many left-leaning policies, this is how they come across, but the policies fail to deliver. Let's just take a look at one of their promises; raising the minimum wage to $15/hr. First, a little context. Hiking the minimum wage in Alberta even up to $11/hr puts it higher than every other province in Canada, and even higher than the Yukon. Hiking it up to $15/hr puts it totally beyond the realm of any other Canadian province by a very significant margin. In fact, according to Wikipedia, $15/hr would move us from being somewhere in the middle of the pack, globally, to being one of the highest paying jurisdictions on the face of the planet, second only to Australia.

But how could that possibly be a bad idea? This would seem to be one example of an obvious way of helping the "little guy."

Well, let's do a little math. Currently in Alberta the minimum wage is pretty close to $10/hr. If somebody has a full-time job[6] at \$10/hr then they'll work approximately 2,000 hrs / year.

$10/hr * 2,000 hr/yr = \$20,000 / yr$

In Alberta the basic personal exemption is about \$18,000, so this person would only have to pay tax on \$2,000 (\$20,000 salary - \$18,000 basic personal exemption).

Now suppose their minimum wage is raised to \$15/hr, keeping everything else the same. The annual income is now \$15 / hr * 2,000 hours = \$30,000. Well, that's much better, isn't it?

Yes, it is much better, not only for the minimum wage worker, but also for the NDP government! After all, if the basic personal exemption is maintained at \$18,000 then this worker is required to pay taxes on \$30,000 - \$18,000 = \$12,000. With the current minimum wage, the NDP would only be able to tax \$2,000, but now they will be able to tax \$12,000. Raising the minimum wage will allow the NDP to take 6X as much tax from minimum wage workers! Does that still sound compassionate?

Some people might think this tax grab is still a good thing because, after all, the poorest still have more after-tax income than before. Technically, yes they do. But let's imagine a company – a flower shop – with several employees who have worked there for differing lengths of time. Their hourly rates will vary according to their work experience.

Crystal	Brand new	\$10/hr
Ed	1 year	\$12/hr

---

[6] From my research it would appear minimum wage workers are typically part time and very young. This is just an example to illustrate some of the consequences of hiking the minimum wage; it is not a precise analysis of real conditions, though the principles remain.

Jenn	2 years	$14/hr
Bob	3 years	$16/hr

With the minimum wage increase, Crystal, Ed and Jenn are all bumped up to $15/hr, at least. But it's not really fair if Ed, who's been there for a year more than Crystal, gets the same salary as Crystal does. And Jenn, likewise, ought to earn more than Ed. And, of course, Bob – at $16/hr – should definitely enjoy more than just a $1/hr benefit over minimum wage if he's already worked at the flower shop for 3 years. If Crystal is starting out at $15/hr then is seems reasonable that Ed would now earn, say, $16 or $17/hr. Jenn should probably be around $18/hr and Bob's wage will probably land somewhere around $20/hr.

With an increase in minimum wage, not only is Crystal's wage increased significantly, so are all the other staff, in the interest of fairness. Raising the minimum wage ends up effectively raising everybody's wages (at least those who are relatively close to minimum wage) so the florist has to deal with a significant increase in their compensation expenses.

Canadian florists[7] spend over 20% of their total revenue on wages, benefits, labour and commission and they only enjoy about 5% net profit. If the flower shop were to try to absorb the minimum wage increase without passing that cost on to their customers, cutting hours or laying anybody off, then the costs associated with wages that used to only take up 20% of revenue would now take up closer to 30% of revenue; an increase of 10% of the total operating costs. Where would that 10% go? The 5% net profit would drop by 10% to become a 5% net loss

---

[7] You'll have to look the data up manually at this site - https://www.ic.gc.ca/app/sme-pme/bnchmrkngtl/rprt-flw.pub?execution=e1s1. Search for NAICS code 453110.

and our poor flower shop would very quickly be out of business. Clearly they have to increase their prices if they want to stay in business without impacting their staff.

But not only has the flower company's compensation costs gone up, so have the compensation costs of the delivery company that transports the flowers to the shop. And so have the compensation costs of the technicians who take care of their refrigeration equipment that keeps the flowers fresh. Same for the company that manages their website. And the company that does their accounting.

And on, and on, and on.

Guess what just happened to the price of flowers in that shop? If the flower shop wants to stay in business then the price of flowers simply must increase as a result of increasing minimum wage. As minimum wage goes up, so does the cost of goods. It will now cost more to buy flowers, food, clothing, houses and pretty much everything else. What good is a pay raise if everything just got more expensive to buy?

But that assumes no changes to staffing. Suppose a manager of a warehouse is allotted $300/hr for staffing, all at minimum wage. If the minimum wage is set at $10/hr then the manager is able to hire 30 staff. However, if the minimum wage is set at $15/hr, then the manager is only able to hire 20 staff. Or, in the worst case, if the manager currently has 30 staff at $10/hr, then when the minimum wage increase is put into effect the manager needs to lay off 10 staff.

But instead of laying people off, business owners could take another approach; reducing hours. So Crystal might have earned $10/hr while working 40 hours per week, but with the minimum wage increase to $15/hr her boss at the flower shop can now only afford to have her come in for about 27 hours each week. So much for the pay hike!

By implementing an increase in minimum wage, the

government is able to take more taxes from the poorest in our province, the poorest may lose their jobs or have their hours cut, and everybody (including the poorest) suddenly must pay more for everything they buy. Does this all still sound compassionate?

But it gets worse, at least for some people. When the cost of living goes up then people with fixed incomes – for instance, seniors who are slowly tapping into their RRSPs – are in trouble. Everybody else can enjoy the benefit of increased wages to offset the increased cost of living, but seniors will be stuck with a less flexible form of income. The NDP made a big deal about helping the elderly, but this policy alone is more likely to make things worse for the elderly than better; their "income" remains the same but everything is suddenly more expensive.

In fact, there is a fascinating correlation between minimum wage and the tendency of people to migrate into, or out of, a province. The provinces with the highest minimum wage should be the most attractive provinces to work in, right? Well, apparently not. As shown in Appendix A, it is the provinces with the lowest minimum wage that have the highest influx of Canadians, and all the other province are losing people. Canadians prefer to move away from progressive provinces and into not-so-progressive provinces. So, once again, if you want to make Alberta the kind of province that people like to visit, but do not want to live in, hiking the minimum wage is one way to get there quickly.

All-in-all, raising the minimum wage is going to have a long list of unintended, and unpleasant, effects that left-leaning politicians either don't think about or don't want to admit. As with so many left-leaning policies it sure sounds reasonable and compassionate, but the results they promise just aren't there.

6 SUMMARY

Left-leaning policies always sounds grander and more compassionate than do right-leaning policies. But history has shown (and ex-Manitobans will confirm) that what sounds good on paper simply does not work out in reality. "Best intentions" end up meeting "the law of unintended consequences." In the case of provinces like Saskatchewan, people eventually wise up and opt for policies that major on realism and minor on ideology over policies that sound compassionate but fail to deliver. In the case of provinces like Manitoba, people just keep moving out, if they are able, and those who are left behind keep on voting for left-leaning parties.

Now please hear me out on this. I'm not claiming that every right-leaning government is automatically good, and always implementing good policies. Certainly not. Right-leaning politicians certainly can mess things up, and they are just as likely as anybody (even left-leaning politicians) to give in to corruption, cronyism, etc. I'm certainly not suggesting we just figure out which political party leans the furthest right and blindly vote for them. It's a lot more complicated than that.

But I am providing a warning here. Left-leaning policies historically do more harm than good. And right-leaning policies, historically, do more good than left-leaning policies. Governments are always run by humans, and political parties are always at risk of human frailty, but right-leaning policies have, on the whole, a significantly better track record than left-leaning policies.

Albertans have a really great province; just ask the steady stream of Canadians who move here from all other parts of Canada. So for the love of Alberta – for the poor in our province, for our families, and for the health of our economy – let's insist on keeping the right-leaning policies that have made this such a great province to live in, work in, and raise our families in.

7 APPENDIX A - ECONOMICS

Using data from various sources including, but not limited to, Canada Revenue Agency and Statistics Canada we can investigate how provincial tax rates (both personal and corporate) and minimum wage are associated with various economic indicators that are used to measure the health of that province's economy. If the progressive ideology is to be believed, then provinces with more progressive economic policies should be healthier. Or, as a minimum, progressive policies should far no worse than their – shall we call them – "regressive" counterparts.

Technical Notes

First, how do we define "progressive" economic policy? Three quintessentially policies are higher income taxes on the wealthy, higher corporate taxes and increased minimum wage. As a quick-and-dirty measure of the personal income tax policy I use something I call the "tax spread" on personal income tax. The tax spread is the difference between the tax rate for the lowest income bracket and the tax rate for the highest income bracket.

Progressive policies favour a greater tax spread; higher tax rates for the wealthy, lower tax rates for the poor.

Until the NDP victory Alberta had a flat tax; the same tax rate of 10% of personal income is paid regardless of income. This would be considered a very "regressive" tax policy. Conversely, the largest tax spread in any Canadian province is found in Nova Scotia where the tax rate on the lowest income bracket is 8.79% and the tax rate on the highest bracket is 21%.

Because the federal tax brackets are the same across all provinces they don't help us compare provinces. Federal taxes are ignored in this book.

In earlier editions of this book I included unemployment data. Upon consideration I have removed this for two reasons. First, unemployment can vary wildly depending on economic conditions that have absolutely nothing to do with economic policies of government, like the plummeting price of oil Alberta experienced in 2015. More importantly, though, oftentimes the unemployed in one province will relocate to another province. Those who have jobs stay. Thus if there are job losses in one province and the unemployed leave then the unemployment rate in the province will necessarily stabilize. The results were fairly chaotic anyway, and that likely explains why.

Interprovincial migration data is shown on a per capita basis; how many people move into / out of the province per 1,000 people already living there. This seems obviously more meaningful than absolute numbers; it isn't really fair to directly compare Ontario to PEI. A positive value means more Canadians are moving in than out.

Similarly, GDP is normalized to the population and presented on a per capita basis in order to more fairly compare PEI to Ontario (etc).

Poverty is notoriously difficult to define and measure

(even Stats Can says so, not just my opinion) so I look at this from two sources. First, there is a website (reference at the end) that attempts to measure poverty but I didn't see how they measured it. Still, they seem to specialize in this so I'll assume their measurement is a good start. Second, I try to indirectly measure poverty by looking at the number of people in the bottom income brackets in each province. I compared the bottom 3 brackets (less than $15K annual income) and the bottom 5 brackets (less than $25K annual income). This is substantially easier to measure, but may not be precisely correlated to poverty. Still, it should be close enough.

The "Market Bread Measure" provided by Statistics Canada estimates the cost of living in various parts of the country. Not only does it break it down by province, it also breaks it down by major centers within the province. That makes it hard to measure apples to apples, or in this case, bread to bread. For this analysis I used the lowest cost in each province as my baseline for comparison.

With respect to poverty data for the USA available on Wikipedia, I used the "2014 poverty rates (includes unrelated children)" because there appears to be an error in the data in the first column. Unless Oregon seriously has a 78.6% poverty rate!

The migration data is fairly sparse prior to 2001 and the data I found only runs up to 2012 so I'll only look at that decade. I considered the most recent year alone, the average of the last 5 years, and the average of the last 10 years. A decade is a long time and a lot can change. Also, a single year, by itself, is a somewhat small sample size. For the below charts I show the five-year average, but the trends remain regardless of the time span you look at.

Poverty / Median Income

Without further adieu, some results. First let's start with the low hanging fruit by comparing tax spread to poverty.

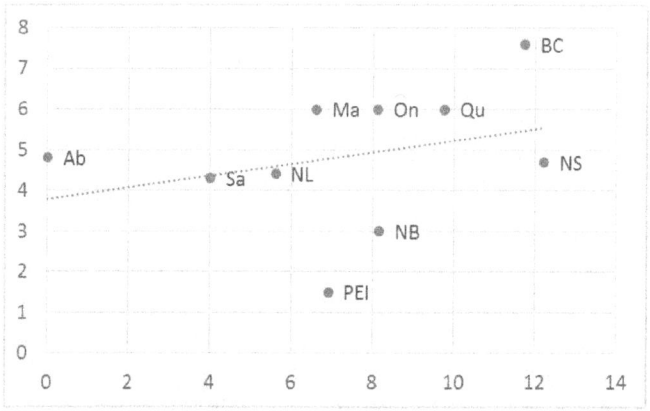

Figure 1 - Poverty Rate vs Income Tax Spread

Along the bottom the tax spread ranges from 0 (Alberta) up to 12.21% (Nova Scotia). Along the vertical axis is the poverty rate, ranging from about 1.5% (PEI) up to almost 8% (BC). Alberta's poverty rate is roughly average for Canada.

As I mentioned in the technical notes, poverty rate is hard to define so there isn't a very strong trend based on this data set. However, the small trend that does present itself shows that as tax spread increases – the more progressive a province is (those on the right side of the chart) – poverty seems to slightly increase as well. In fact, BC has the highest poverty rate (almost 8% on the vertical axis) and one of the most progressive tax policies (almost 12% tax spread on the horizontal axis).

But let's look at the low income bracket approach I mentioned in the technical notes.

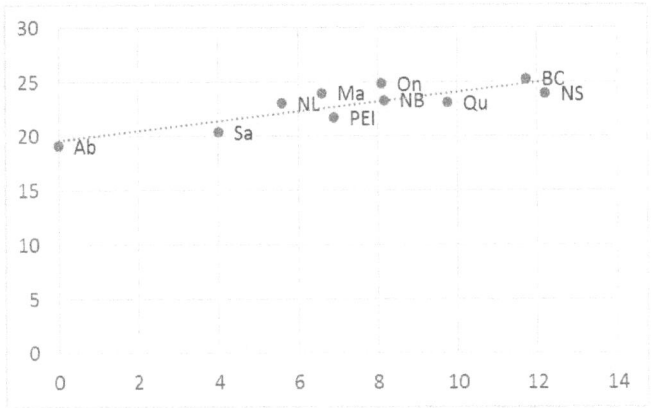

Figure 2 - Percent in Low Income vs Income Tax Spread

With the same tax spread info along the bottom axis you can see a much clearer trend regarding how many people are in low income situations (less than $15K annual income). The change doesn't appear to be massive – only about 5% - but when you remember that Canada has a total population of over 30M people, 5% becomes a bit more significant. As with poverty, the more progressive a province's income tax policy the higher the percent of people who only earn the lowest income tax brackets. Alberta has the lowest number of people in the low income brackets. As with the previous chart BC retains its position as the province with the highest percent of people in the lowest income brackets.

In fact, let's consider this from a different perspective. Is there a correlation between tax policy and median income in the province? Indeed there is, as shown below.

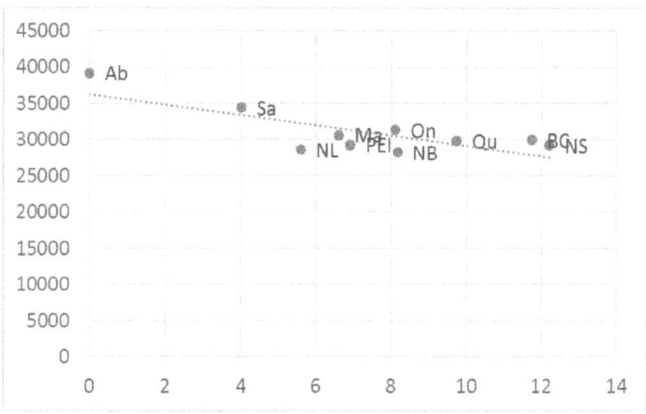

Figure 3 - Median Income vs Income Tax Spread

This relationship is the inverse of the previous one; as a province adopts more progressive tax policies its citizens tend to earn a lower median income. And the difference between the highest earning province and the lowest earning province is about $10K per year, or roughly 1/3 of the median income. How would you enjoy a 33% pay raise? Alberta, again on the far left of the chart, has the highest median income in Canada.

Ok, so what if we consider the income tax rates directly, instead of the income tax spread? Do those provinces that drop the tax rate for the lowest income bracket see a reduction of people in that tax bracket?

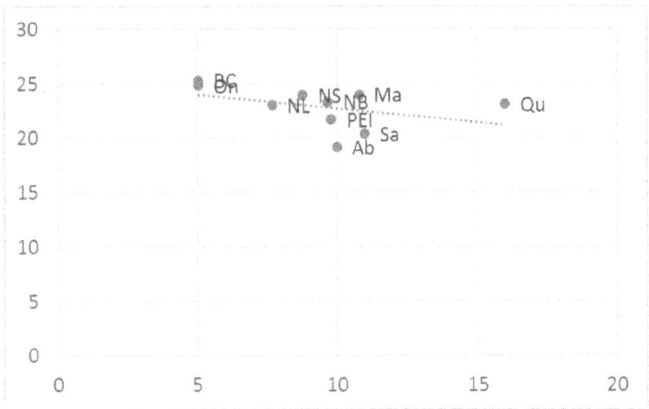

Figure 4 - Percent in Low Income vs Low Income Tax Rate

The correlation clearly isn't all that strong, but it would seem that the best way to reduce the number of people in the low income bracket (the vertical axis) would be to increase the tax rate on the low income bracket (bottom axis). In short, progressive policies do not appear to help raise people out of low income (i.e. poverty) situations. If it seems strange that higher income tax on the lowest income earners would be associated with fewer low income earners then you are in for a real mind job next.

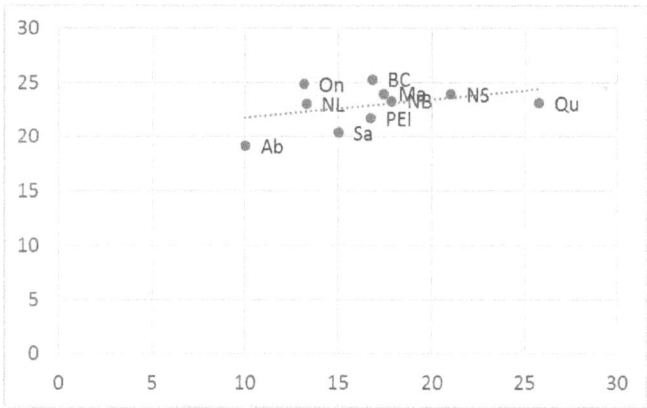

Figure 5 - Percent in Low Income vs High Income Tax Rate

I bet you didn't see this one coming. As you increase the tax rate on the highest income earners (i.e. the wealthiest) you end up getting a larger percent of people in the low income bracket, though the trend is somewhat weaker. This may not make immediate sense if you adhere to a progressive ideology, but make no mistake about the fact that this is what the data shows.

In short, the economic policy most associated with fewer people in low income situations is relatively higher taxes on the lowest income earners and relatively lower tax on the highest income earners. Put another way, governments should reduce or eliminate the tax spread. Alberta had it right with the flat tax.

But that's personal income tax; what about corporate taxes? Left-leaning policies tend to expect the corporate world to "contribute a little more" as the NDP platform described it (section 6.1). Do provinces with higher corporate tax rates tend to have higher median income or lower median income for the general population? Unfortunately, lower, as the following chart shows.

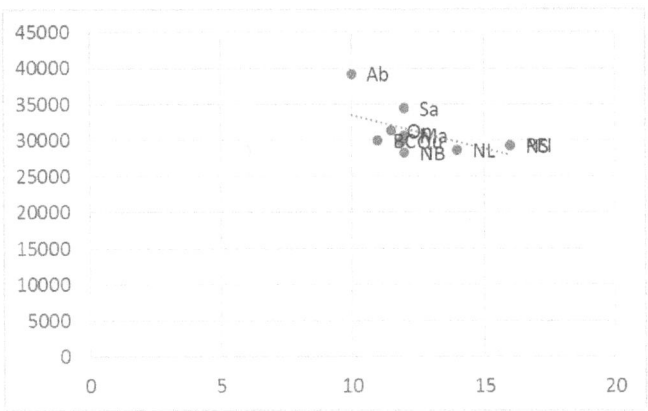

Figure 6 - Median Income vs Corporate Tax Rate

The corporate tax rate (not for small businesses) is shown on the bottom axis and the median income in the province is shown on the vertical axis. The general trend shows that provinces with the highest corporate tax rate for corporations also tend to have the lower median income for people in the province. I will be the first to admit that the correlation isn't as strong as the personal income tax rates. Excluding two of the higher provinces on the left, the data is almost flat. But it is interesting that the two provinces with the highest median income also have some of the lowest corporate tax rates.

But what about tax breaks for small businesses? This would be analogous to the tax spread for personal income as described earlier. Does a large "corporate tax spread" improve the situation for citizens? Actually, no, as the following chart shows.

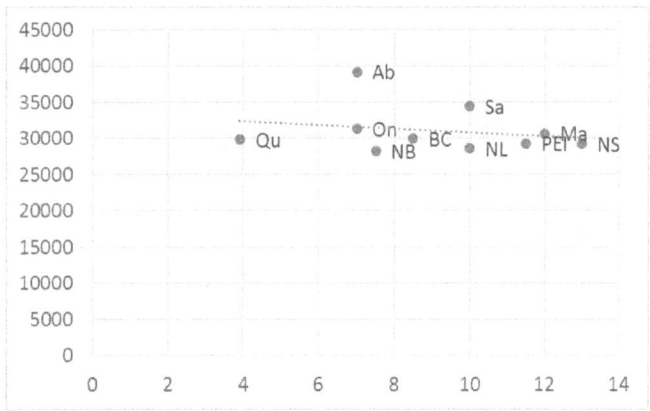

Figure 7 - Median Income vs Corporate Tax Spread

The data is a bit more scattered, but a larger corporate tax spread is associated with almost no change in median income. If anything, increasing the corporate tax spread seems to marginally reduce the median income, though the correlation is quite weak and I wouldn't draw any far-reaching conclusions from it. In short, this particular progressive policy either makes no real difference to median income, at best, or it slightly reduces it, at worst.

In summary, giving tax breaks to small businesses isn't nearly as helpful as just keeping all the corporate tax rates as low as possible. If anything, corporate tax spread is associated with lower median income for the general population.

The last progressive policy I mentioned is minimum wage. How does an increase in minimum wage impact the economic indicators of a province? To start with, let's consider how many people are in low income bracket as a function of minimum wage.

[One quick note. Minimum wage does not vary significantly from province to province. The following observations are very general and I try to avoid sweeping conclusions based on such narrow variation.]

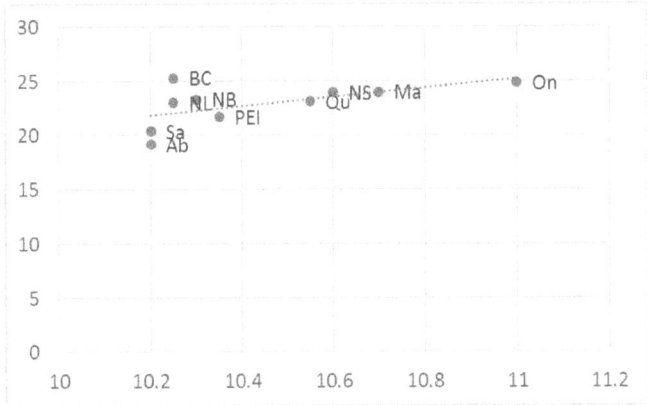

Figure 8 - Percent Low Income vs Minimum Wage

As this chart shows, the provinces with higher minimum wage (further to the right on the horizontal axis) also tend to have more people in low income bracket (further up the vertical axis). This may seem a little ironic considering how much emphasis is given to the importance of minimum wage increases in helping people on the lowest end of the income spectrum. The impact of progressive policies does not seem to be nearly as positive as they presumably hope those policies will be.

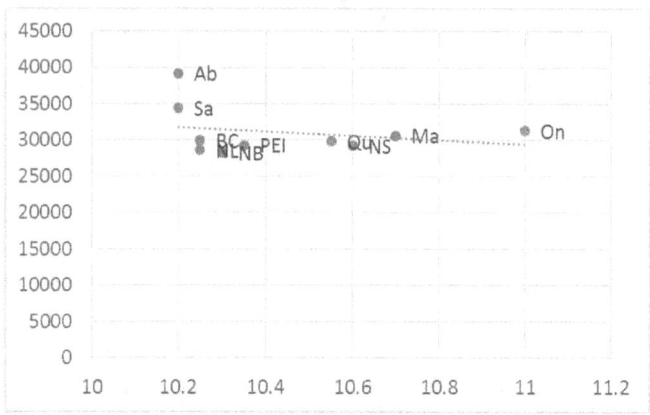

Figure 9 - Median Income vs Minimum Wage

Relatedly, and probably not surprisingly given the previous chart, median income also drops in provinces with higher minimum wage as the above chart shows. This one, though, is admittedly far less strongly correlated. With the exception of two outliers (Ab and Sa) it is virtually flat. So at best, an increase in minimum wage does not seem to increase the median income.

Gross Domestic Product

GDP is the total value of all goods and services produced by a province. It's a pretty good measure of just how economically active a province is; higher GDP means people are buying and selling more goods and services. More sales would seem to suggest more jobs, and so on. So another question we should ask is whether progressive policies are associated with a higher or lower GDP.

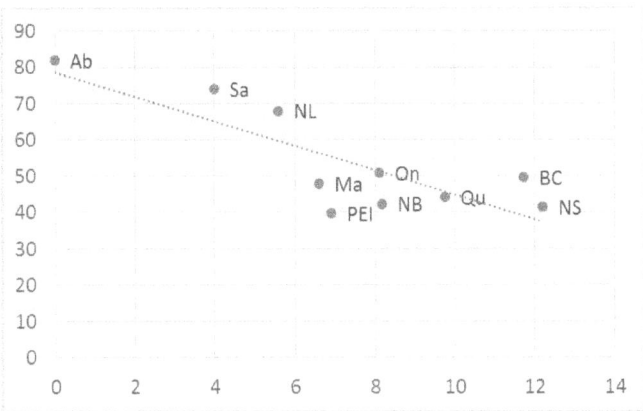

Figure 10 - GDP vs Tax Spread

The above chart shows the Per Capita GDP in each of the provinces on the vertical axis and the tax spread on the horizontal axis. Of all the correlations I examined this was one of the strongest and clearest. As the tax spread is increased in a province – as it implements increasingly progressive economic policies – the Per Capita Gross Domestic Product drops. And the magnitude of the drop is very significant; a factor of 2 between the highest and the lowest. We might be inclined to consider that other factors are at play, in particular to size of the province. First of all, the fact that I converted GDP to "per capita" functionally eliminates that variable. But to verify that population isn't a factor please note that Ontario and PEI – the largest and smallest provinces in Canada, respectively – are very close to each other on the chart!

The story gets more interesting, though. What if we compare the tax rate on the highest and lowest earners to GDP?

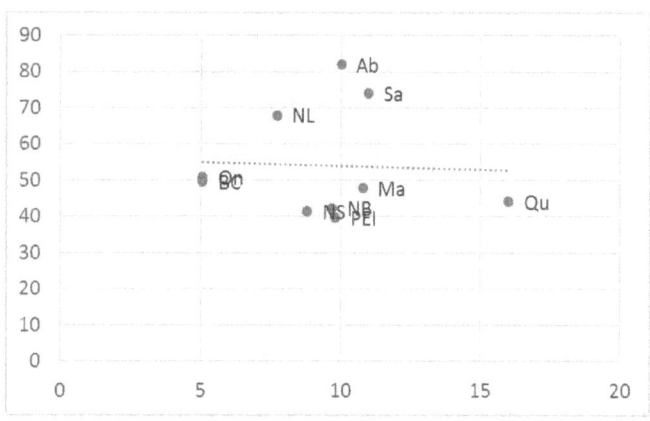

Figure 11 - GDP vs Lowest Tax Rate

As this chart shows, changing the tax rate on the lowest income earners does not seem to significantly impact the GDP of the province. But if the tax spread impacts GDP, and the impact is negligible on the lowest income earners, then there must be a correlation with the highest income earners, right?

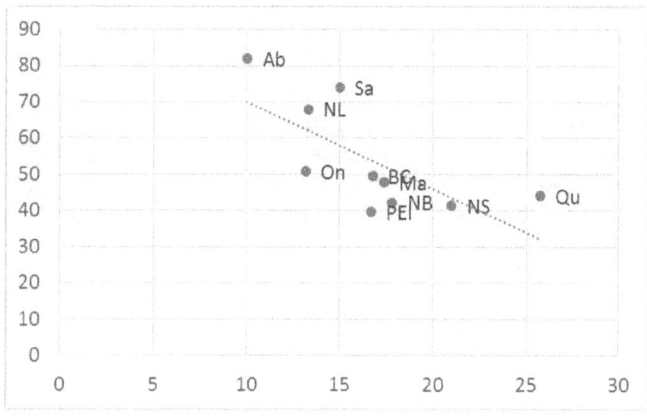

Figure 12 - GDP vs Highest Tax Rate

Indeed there is, as the above chart shows. As you

increase the tax rate on the highest income earners you can clearly see that the GDP drops significantly. So if the above data is accurate then you can positively impact GDP (and the overall economic health of the province) by reducing the taxes on the highest income earners, and narrowing the gap between the tax rate of the highest income earners and the lowest income earners.

You may have heard of something called the "trickle-down" theory of economics. The idea is simple; if a person has more money to spend, they are likely to spend it. Thus the accumulation of wealth by the highest income earners ends up having a net positive impact on society because they spend the money they have earned. Not all of it – this is obviously a simplification of a more complicated theory – but that's the general concept.

The above chart appears to confirm this trend. As a government takes more money from the wealthy it necessarily reduces the amount of wealth that they are able to spend in the province. And the fact that the GDP of the province similarly drops seems to strongly imply that trickle-down economics is a highly plausible contributing factor. Trickle-down economics is not the whole story, of course, but it is a factor that cannot be ignored.

In fact, the correlation between disposable income and GDP in a province seems undeniable in light of the correlation between sales tax and GDP. Sales tax is another means by which government reduces the amount of disposable income citizens have to spend – right at the cash register – so the impact ought to be similar even though it targets all spenders, regardless of income. The following chart confirms this.

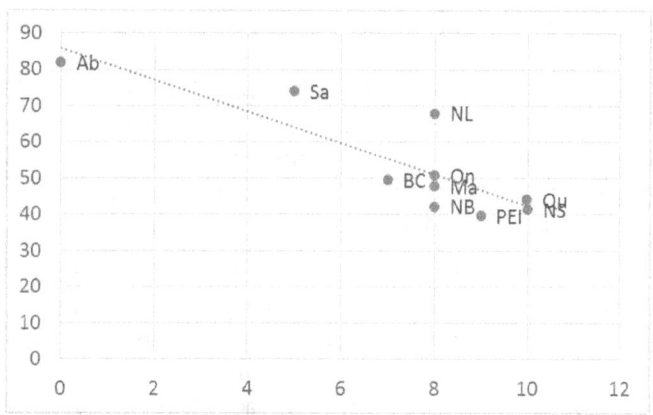

Figure 13 - GDP vs Sales Tax

Clearly the higher the sales tax in the province the lower the sales that one can expect to see.

In the interest of space I won't provide all the charts, but increased sales tax is associated with the same negative indicators that the other progressive policies have:

- Lower median income

- More people in low income bracket

- More people want to move out of the provinces with higher sales tax

I haven't provided data about interprovincial migration patterns yet so let's take a look at that next.

Interprovincial Migration

Measuring various factors is one interesting way of considering how beneficial this or that policy is to the citizens in a province, but another measure is to consider whether people want to live in that province or not. We can analyze to our heart's content, but the feet on the ground tell the real story of how desirable it is to live somewhere. Fortunately, Statistics Canada provides interprovincial migration data for us to analyze. This is data about where people already living in Canada move to / from, not where new arrivals to our country settle down.

Are the interprovincial migration patterns in Canada correlated with the tax spread and the median income? Indeed they are. The larger the tax spread – the more progressive the province is – the more likely people are to move out (as shown in the chart below).

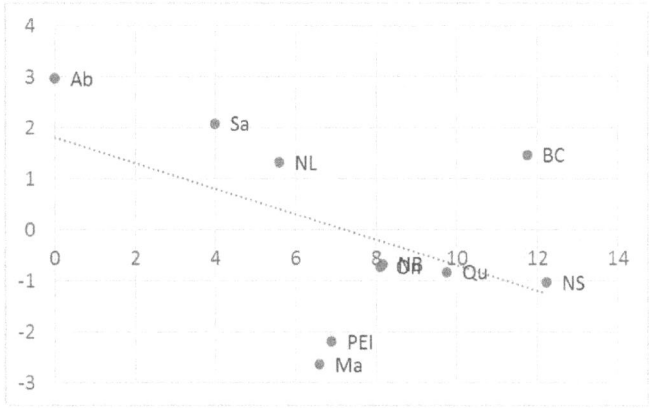

Figure 14 - Interprovincial Migration vs Tax Spread

And, similarly, the greater the median income, the more likely people are to move in, as shown in the chart below.

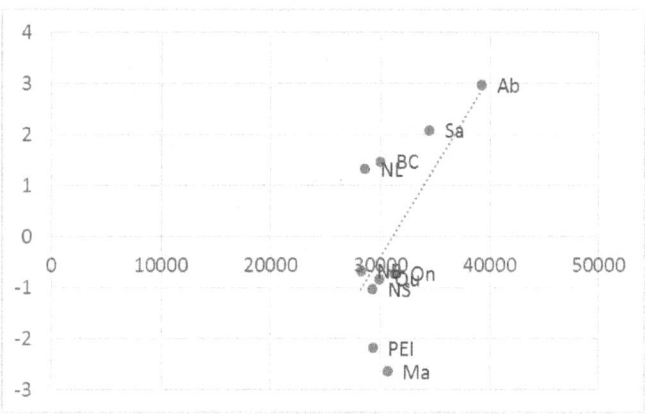

Figure 15 - Interprovincial Migration vs Median Income

Lastly, the lower the minimum wage (lower, not higher) the more likely people are to want to move into the province. People actually want to move out of provinces with higher minimum wages!

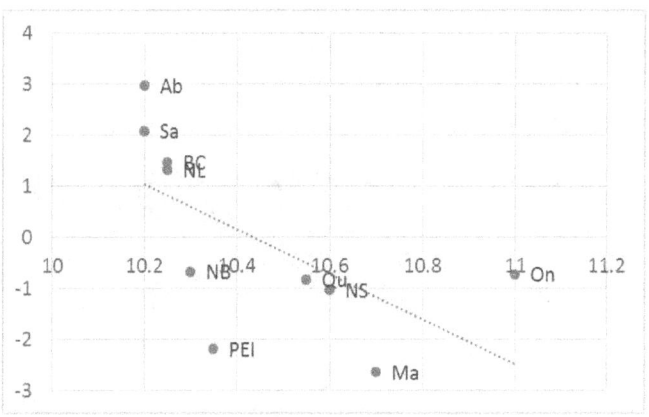

Figure 16 - Interprovincial Migration vs Minimum Wage

It hardly seems likely that people are moving to provinces with lower minimum wages because they are seeking lower income (the previous chart would strongly suggest otherwise). It seems more plausible that a lower minimum wage means greater availability of work because employees are able to hire more people at a lower rate. Whatever the explanation, though, it seems clear that this is another progressive policy that Canadians are apparently not attracted to.

Cost of living factor

As I said earlier in the book there is little benefit to having a higher income if the cost of living in the province happens to be higher. Although minimum wage is not widely divergent across Canada (yet), and is therefore very unlikely to impact the cost of living, other factors do introduce some variability. Measuring the cost of living isn't exactly an easy thing to do because so many factors are at play. Statistics Canada uses something called the "Market Bread Measure" to roughly compare the cost of living in various parts of the country. It would seem there isn't a strong correlation between median income and the cost of living, as the following chart shows.

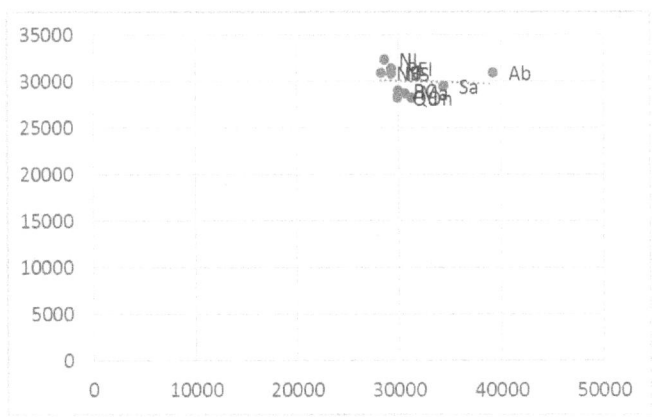

Figure 17 - Market Bread Measure vs Median Income

It would seem that it is possible to actually enjoy the benefits of increased income (if it isn't due to the effects of dramatic minimum wage increases, at least) without suffering from artificially inflated cost of living. With that extra money, who knows, maybe you could help increase GDP.

What about the USA?

Ok, so this is some interesting data for Canada, but do our neighbours to the South see the same effect? I found data a little harder to come by, but I did dig up some information worth considering. And with 50 states, that's 5X the work to analyze, so this is just a quick snapshot.

The Institute on Taxation and Economic Policy (ITEP) publishes a fascinating document called "Who pays?" In their document they politely demonize certain states by showing that they have more "regressive" tax policies than other states. They measure this by comparing the percent tax paid by the top 1% earners to the percent tax paid by the bottom 20% earners. They divide the tax burden for the bottom 20% by the tax burden for the top 1% and, lo and behold, in some states the poorest suffer 7X the tax burden as the wealthiest do!!!!

Yes, you read that right! The poor pay up to 7X more relative tax than the wealthiest do. Where is the justice?!?!

Now if that strikes you as a little odd, it struck me as a little odd too. Read the fine print, folks.

The report includes a section describing the "economic case for tax fairness" in which it claims that states with more progressive tax structures will enjoy higher tax revenues. Regressive tax structures, conversely, "prevent states from investing in the priorities that will bolster the prospects of low- and middle-income residents." In short, the government needs the tax money in order to address the poverty problem.

So, being the inquisitive guy that I am, I thought it would be interesting to compare the "regressive" ratio (tax on the poorest 20% divided by the tax on the top 1%) to the poverty rate in each of these states, said information being readily available on Wikipedia. The following chart shows that comparison according to one of the sets of data provided.

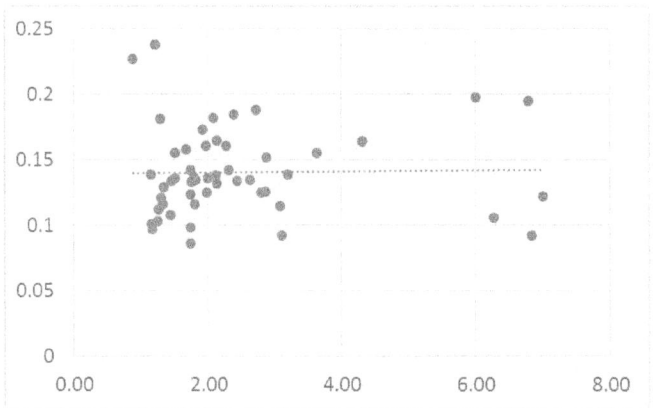

Figure 18 - Poverty rate (1) vs Regressive Tax Ratio

Multiple measures of poverty are provided at Wikipedia, so the following chart shows the same data but with one of the other measures of poverty.

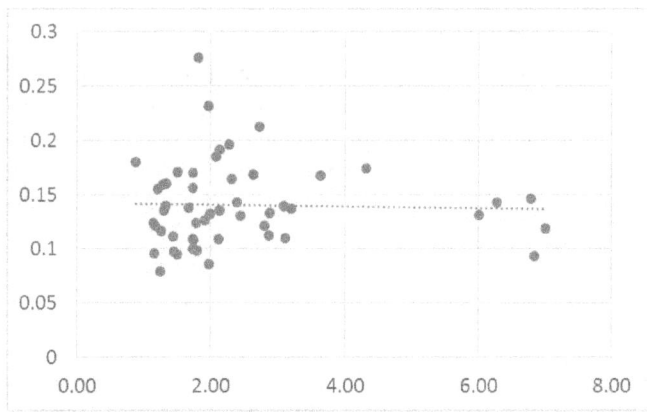

Figure 19 - Poverty rate (2) vs Regressive Tax Ratio

There seems to be very little correlation between how regressive a state's tax structure is, and how prevalent poverty is in that state. Indeed, some of the most regressive states (the ones on the far right) have relatively low poverty rates. Conversely, the states with the highest poverty rates (in excess of 20%, for instance) have relatively progressive tax structures. In short, progressive tax policy, at best, has no real impact on poverty.

But that should hardly come as a surprise, considering what I've already shown to be the case in Canada.

I combed through the data to find any real correlations between various taxes and poverty but I mostly came up dry. With so many states and such variability between their tax policies (did you know some state have zero income tax!) most of the charts looked like they were used for target practice. The futility of my search does seem to strongly imply that whatever kinds of economic policies you implement, they are unlikely to have a significant impact on poverty. It's like poverty isn't, fundamentally, a problem about money. Sound familiar?

The only other modest correlation that surfaced was between the Sales & Excise tax burden on the lowest 20%

and the poverty rate. Based on the data we've seen so far this shouldn't come as any surprise.

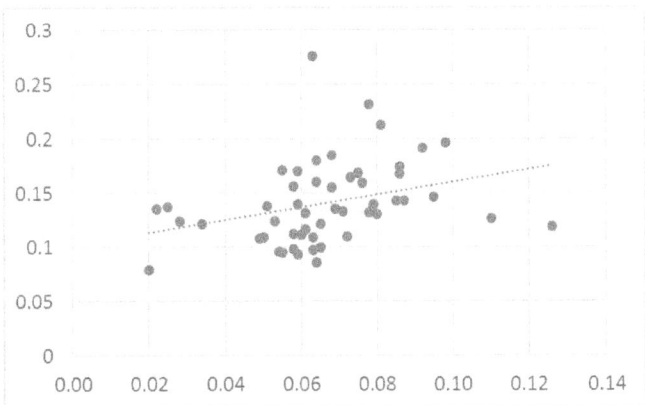

Figure 20 - Poverty Rate vs S&E tax burden on bottom 20%

Once again higher taxes (further right on the horizontal axis) is somewhat correlated with an increase in poverty (vertical axis).

Charitable giving

So the thrust of all this data seems to point to one reality; progressive economic policies that intend to help the poor and the lowest income earners doesn't seem to provide the intended results. Lower taxes and smaller government seems to do a better job. But how can that be? How can a smaller government with fewer resources at its disposal be more effective in lifting people out of poverty?

Maybe it's because the government isn't the one doing the job of lifting people out of poverty. Corporations that provide jobs are a massive contributing factor, so long as government doesn't saddle them with unnecessarily large tax burdens. But there's something else going on here too, and that's with private charities. And this is where our last analysis comes in; how does charitable giving differ from province to province? More specifically, how is charitable giving related to various economic indicators?

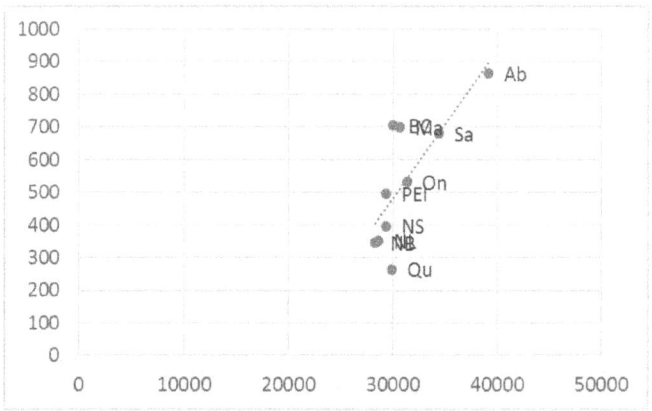

Figure 21 - Annual Charitable Giving vs Median Income

The first chart tells a lot; as median income goes up (further right on the horizontal axis) so does the average annual charitable giving in the province (vertical axis). It would seem higher earners are higher givers.

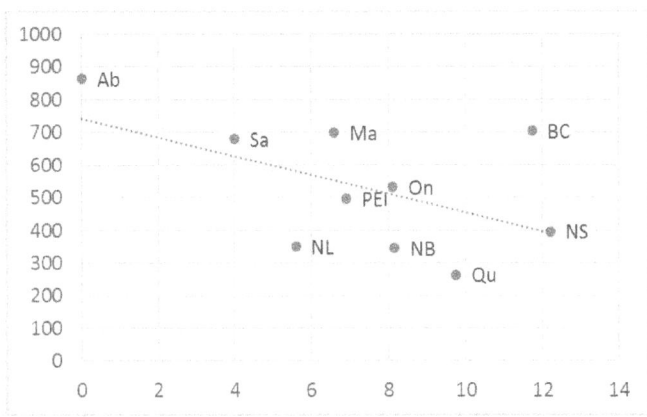

Figure 22 - Annual Charitable Giving vs Tax Spread

The above chart shows something interesting; as tax spread increases (i.e. as the province is more progressive) then charitable giving appears to drop. This correlation is a bit more scattered, but the trend seems clear.

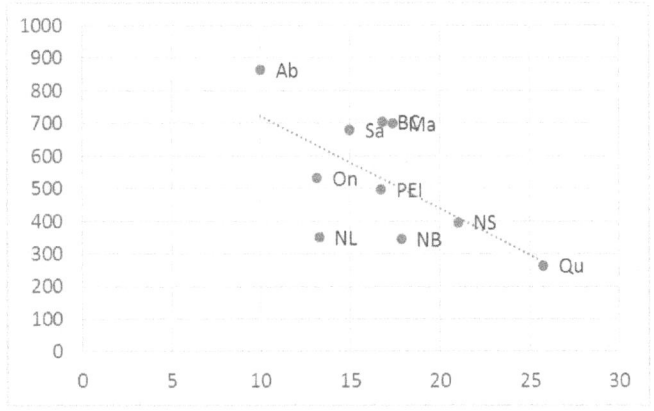

Figure 23 - Charitable Giving vs Highest Tax Rate

This one is also interesting; as you increase the tax rate on the highest income earners that charitable giving drops. I guess the theory of trickle-down economics applies not only to purchases of goods and services but also to charitable giving; as the government takes more money people are more inclined to keep what's left.

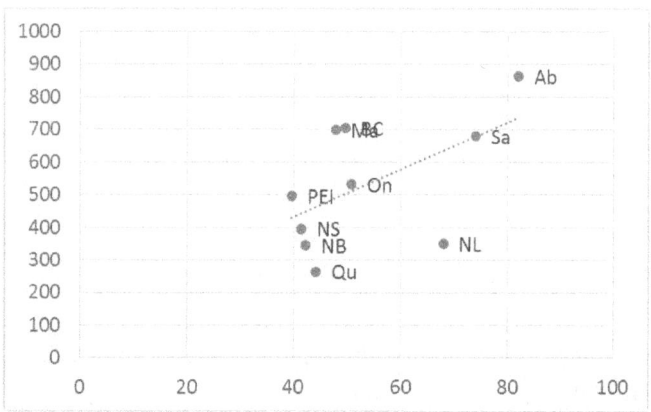

Figure 24 - Charitable Giving vs GDP

Related to the previous point, as the GDP of a province increases (further right on the horizontal axis) – in short, how economically vibrant the province is – the more generous its citizens tend to be.

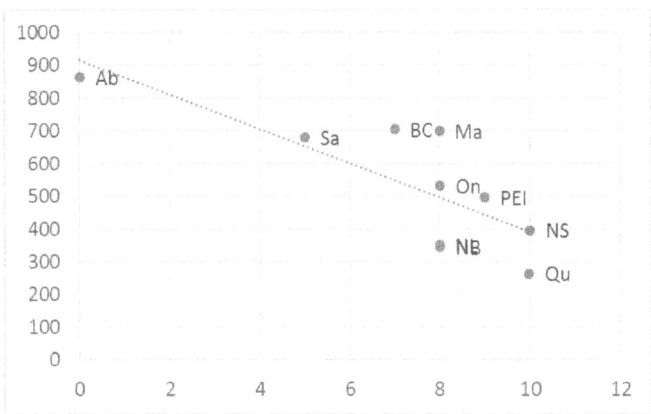

Figure 25 - Charitable Giving vs Provincial Sales Tax

One last one; provincial sales tax. As a province's sales tax increases (further right on the horizontal axis) then the charitable giving of its citizens declines.

In short, as a province strives to embrace a more progressive economic policy, its citizens are more inclined to hold on to whatever money the government "allows" them to keep. They are less likely to donate to charity. It's not hard to imagine that the thinking might go along the lines of "it's not my job to help, it's the government's; that's why we pay taxes."

Commentary

It would seem to me that the most generous interpretation one can draw from the above data is that progressive economic policies are not associated with improved economic conditions in a province. But that is being very generous. A more realistic assessment is that progressive economic policies are associated with lower income, more people in low-income situations, lower GDP, more poverty, less charitable generosity from the citizens and a greater likelihood that people are going to wand to relocate out of the province.

Naturally, correlation does not equal causation. It is possible that changing the minimum wage, introducing "progressive" tax regimes and taxing large corporations is not the cause of lower income and higher migration patterns. While the plausibility seems high to me, one cannot technically say, for certain, that these are the causes. Fair enough.

However, what we should be able to say for certain is that, given the consistent trends shown here, the government should be extremely cautious before implementing these kinds of policies. If progressive policies are not to blame, what is? And why is it that economic misfortune is so often found wherever progressive policies are implemented? Clearly this deserves careful consideration and extreme caution from politicians.

Data sources

Tax rate in Canada:

http://www.cra-arc.gc.ca/tx/ndvdls/fq/txrts-eng.html

Income level in Canada:

http://www.statcan.gc.ca/tables-tableaux/sum-som/l01/cst01/famil105a-eng.htm

Unemployment (April 2015) in Canada:

http://www.statcan.gc.ca/tables-tableaux/sum-som/l01/cst01/lfss01a-eng.htm

Corporate tax data: in Canada

http://www.albertacanada.com/business/overview/competitive-corporate-taxes.aspx

Market Bread Measure in Canada:

http://www.statcan.gc.ca/pub/75f0002m/2012002/tbl
/tbl04-eng.htm

Interprovincial migration in Canada:

http://www.statcan.gc.ca/pub/91-209-
x/2014001/article/14012/tbl/tbl1-eng.htm

Minimum wage in Canada:

http://www.retailcouncil.org/quickfacts/minimum-
wage

Data on the "regressive" American tax structures (see more data in the Appendix links at the bottom):

http://www.itep.org/whopays/full_report.php

Poverty rate in American states:

https://en.wikipedia.org/wiki/List_of_U.S._states_by_
poverty_rate

Poverty rate per Canadian province:

http://www.cpj.ca/files/docs/poverty-trends-
scorecardpdf

Market Bread Measure:

http://www.statcan.gc.ca/pub/75f0002m/2012002/tbl
/tbl04-eng.htm

8 APPENDIX B – FAMILY AND KIDS

Much of the following research relates to cohabitation (living "common law") and the associated "cohabitation effect" that sociologists have observed. The cohabitation effect is so prevalent and so well established that it has its own term! The following data sources are just a snapshot of the plethora of data pointing to the superiority of traditional so-called "nuclear" families for the overall health of children.

In the opening paragraph of this study from 2010 (University of Denver - http://www.ncbi.nlm.nih.gov/pmc/articles/PMC2904561 /) the authors note that "the cohabitation effect related to first marriages is a widely replicated finding." In other words, the cohabitation effect is a broadly accepted reality in the world of sociology, not some crackpot theory. The authors describe some of the general trends of this family arrangement including "negative interactions" and a "greater probability of divorce."

This paper, from the American College of Pediatricians (https://www.acpeds.org/the-college-speaks/position-statements/societal-issues/cohabitation-part-1-of-2) provides significantly more (and frightening) data on cohabiting couples and single-parent families. Here's a sample:

1) The incidence of violence among married couples is between 15% and 31%, whereas the incidence of violence among cohabiting couples is between 22% and 43%.

2) "After controlling for other factors, cohabiters were more than twice as likely to engage in infidelity as married people."

3) "Compared with children in single households or cohabiting families, children in nuclear families have about half the learning disabilities and attention deficit hyperactivity disorder, less behavior problems, less definite or severe emotional or behavior problems, and fewer parents describe their children as worried."

4) "Children reared in an intact family, by both of their biological parents, are statistically less likely to commit a minor or serious crime compared to all other family living arrangements (single mom, single dad, biological dad married to step-mom, or biological mom married to step-dad.)"

One of the largest studies in this area is described at the "family outcomes" website - http://www.familystructurestudies.com/outcomes/. According to virtually every indicator, married biological families have the best outcomes for children.

The American Center for Disease Control published some findings in a document entitled, "Family Structure and Children's Health in the United States." (http://www.cdc.gov/nchs/data/series/sr_10/sr10_246.pdf) As with some of the previously cited research, the list of data is very long so what follows are a few quick snapshots. As is shown in Figures 9 through 27 the "nuclear" family (defined as "one or more children living with two parents who are married to one another and are each biological or adoptive parents to all children in the family") consistently provides the best overall results for children. Some examples include health (measured by various indicators), behavior, anxiety, emotional / behavioral difficulties and missed days of school. With very few exceptions (i.e. Figure 12 – hay fever) children in other family structures (such as cohabiting parents) almost always had more problems.

In a document entitled "domestic violence handbook" provided by Alberta Justice, one of the many common risk factors for domestic homicide is "victim and perpetrator living common-law." (page 116) Yes, you read that right; common law couples are more likely to try and kill each other!

https://justice.alberta.ca/programs_services/families/documents/domesticviolencehandbook.pdf

The need for actively involved fathers is a more recent discovery of sociology. According to this introduction to a book on fathers, "researchers have amassed a solid body of evidence regarding the benefits of positive father involvement for children's wellbeing" (http://media.johnwiley.com.au/product_data/excerpt/14/04712316/0471231614.pdf). The introductory chapter describes some of this body of evidence. It would seem that children do not merely need good "parents," they specifically need a good mom and a good dad! Hence the importance of life-long, stable marriage of the child's biological parents.

Data from Calgary

Ok, so all this information is interesting, in theory, but can we see some real numbers? Yes, we can, and I'll use the city of Calgary to provide some numbers. Demographic information about each of the communities in Calgary is available from the City of Calgary website and crime data for each community in Calgary is available from the Calgary police website. All the data presented below is taken straight from these websites.

City of Calgary community profiles - http://www.calgary.ca/CSPS/CNS/Pages/Research-and-strategy/Community-profiles/Community-Profiles.aspx

Calgary police crime statistics - http://www.calgary.ca/cps/Pages/Statistics/Calgary-Police-statistical-reports.aspx

First some technical background on my calculations. Sorry if this bores you, but people need to know I'm not intentionally skewing the data. If you don't care, you can skip a couple of pages.

I checked crime data from multiple years because some of the years are incomplete. Preference was given to 2013 data, the most recent year with complete data. I did spot check the results against 2012 (also complete) and 2014 and 2015 which were not complete; there is broad consistency.

Also, because I have a day job and a life I didn't cross reference every type of crime against every piece of demographic information for every community in Calgary. I investigated 9 demographic indicators in 34 of Calgary's communities. The total population of those 34 communities represents roughly ¼ of the total population of the city. I tried to draw on communities from all quadrants of the city, and all kinds of socio-economic flavours. That's enough info to see general trends and confirm that the observations made in the above-mentioned scholarly references are actually being lived out in our backyard.

The crime data is presented as a rate per 1,000 people to account for the fact that some communities have vastly larger populations than other communities. The community profiles present marital data first by what percent are with a partner / spouse and how many are not, and then break it down to married / common-law (for those with) and single, separated, divorced or widowed (for those without). To compare indicators more closely, I scaled the values. For instance, in Martindale (where we used to live) the percent of people not living with a spouse / partner is 35%. Of those, 7% are separated and 12% are divorced. For my analysis, the "separated / divorced" number would show up as:

$$\text{Sep / div} = 35\% * (7\% + 12\%) = 6.65\%$$

I also wanted to check some socio-economic indicators that are unrelated to our families. For instance, some people might be concerned that a lot of the social ills we face in Canada are due to the high influx of immigrants in our midst, so I checked that out. Crime data generally shows a negative correlation between the population of immigrants in a community and the crime. The chart below is one example of the negative trend; as a community has more immigrants it tends to have fewer thefts from vehicles though the data is somewhat scattered.

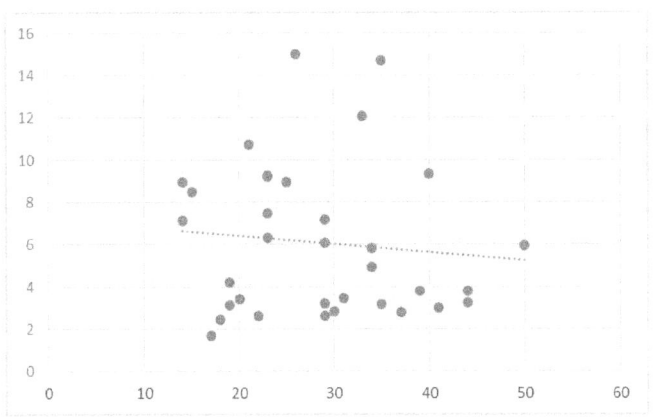

Figure 26 - Theft from Vehicle rate vs Percent Immigrant

The correlation is weak, at best. While the trend points downward, you can see that the data is rather scattered. In brief, there isn't really a strong correlation between the number of immigrants in a community and the crime in the community. If Calgary has any problems it seems unlikely the newcomers are to blame!

Enough technical details, let's get back to the main point; families.

<u>Crime</u>

The data here was a lot more consistent, and confirms what the previously cited studies generally conclude; deviating from the "married biological parents" model for families isn't good. For instance, let's start with the crime of non-domestic assault.

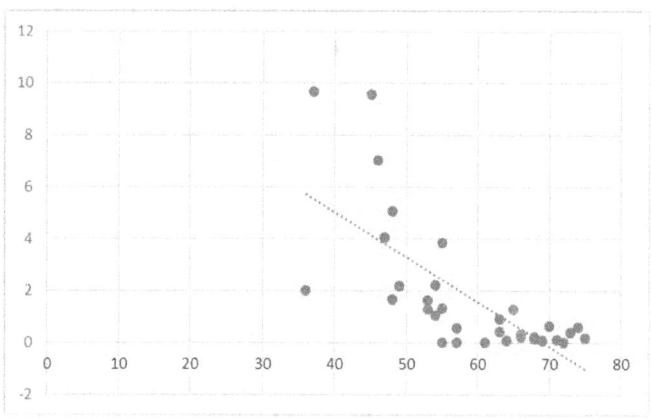

Figure 27 - Non-Domestic Assault vs Percent Marital

As this chart shows, the more couples are in a "marital" relationship (both common-law and married combined – further right on the horizontal axis) the lower the rate of non-domestic assault in the community. But what if we break out married couples from common-law couples?

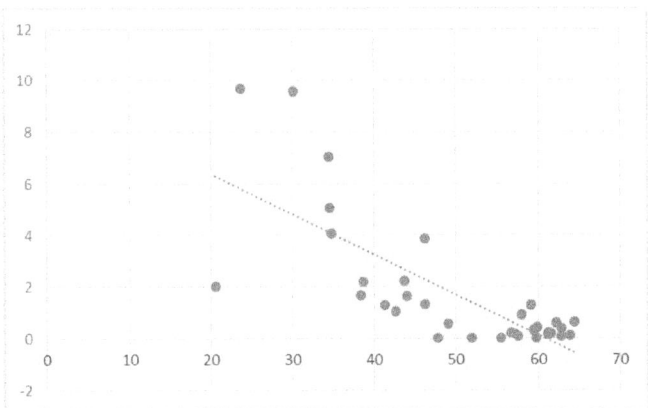

Figure 28 - Non-Domestic Assault vs Percent Married

The trend looks remarkably similar to the previous one, but we have to consider scale. For most communities the percent of "marital" couples that are common-law is relatively low so Married couples will outweigh the common-law couples by virtue of how many of them there are. But what is we break out the common-law factor alone?

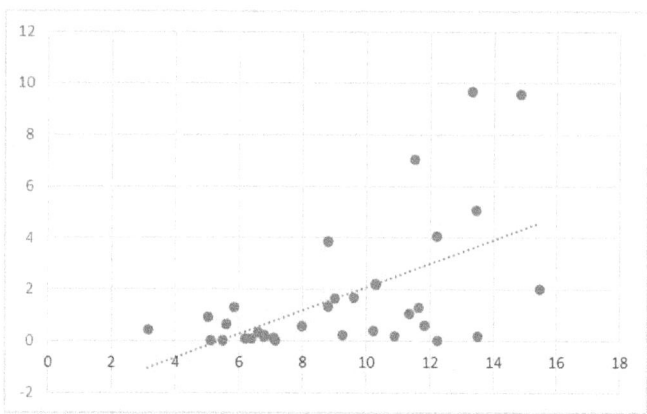

Figure 29 - Non-Domestic Assault vs Percent Common-Law

Now isn't that interesting; the trend reverses itself. As a community has a higher percent of couples living common-law (further right on the horizontal axis) the rate of non-domestic assaults increases. So what happens when couples break up? According to the literature this is a very negative event for kids and adults alike, so does Calgary's crime data show a correlation between the percent of people who are separated or divorced and the crime in the community?

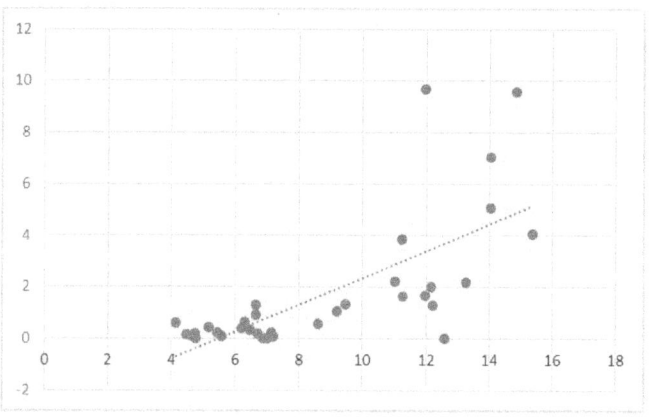

Figure 30 - Non-Domestic Assault vs Percent Separated / Divorced

That correlation seems pretty clear to me. As with common-law couples, as a community has a higher percent of people who are separated or divorced the rate of crime increases. And as couples break up there will be more single parents (if they had kids). Theoretically there should be a correlation between crime and the percent of single parents, right?

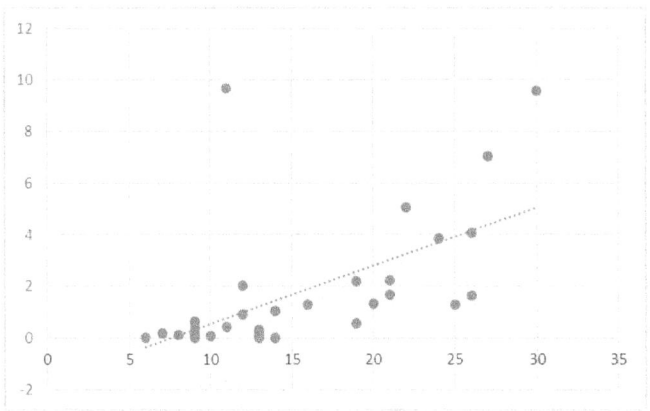

Figure 31 - Non-Domestic Assault vs Percent Lone Parent

Indeed, the correlation remains.

So of all the family arrangements it seems clear that the traditional marriage relationship seems to be best for the health of communities, as confirmed by the literature I previously cited. But that's just one type of crime, what about the others? Of all the types of crime provided by the Calgary Police (assault, robbery, break and enter, disorder, etc) every one of them that I checked, in every year that data is available for, showed the same trends across the board. Only one or two almost didn't show a trend, one of which was commercial break and enter as it correlated to lone parents, especially in 2012 as shown below.

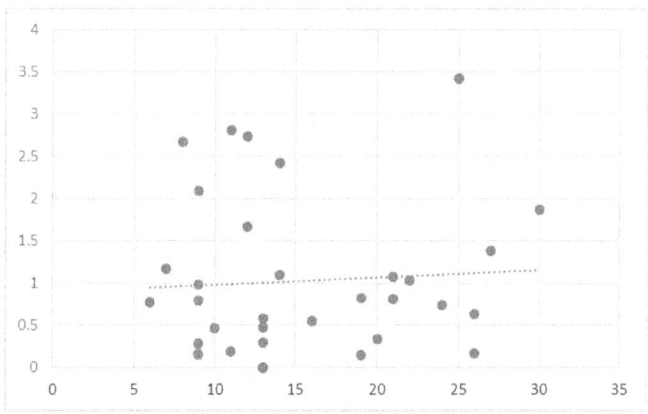

Figure 32 - Commercial B&E (2012) vs Percent Lone Parent

The other correlations that I checked were much clearer and gave universal preference to married family relationships.

I also investigated the correlations between lack of education (high school or beyond) and crime, as well as unemployment and crime.

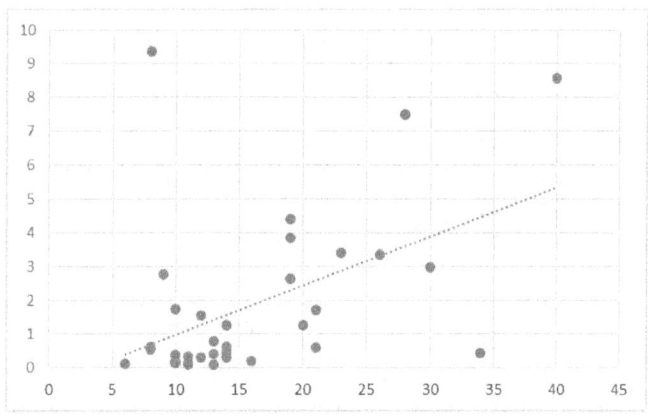

Figure 33 - Non-Domestic Assault vs Percent No High School

As the above chart shows, as the proportion of people in a community without even a high school diploma increases (further right on the horizontal axis) so does the rate of non-domestic assault in that community. Unemployment data is far more variable (as discussed in the previous appendix) but the trend holds for that variable as well; higher unemployment is associated with more crime.

Social Indicators

But that raises an interesting question; is there a correlation between the family stability within communities and the education and employment of those who live in the communities? If the above mentioned research (including that referenced by the magazine published by Alberta Health Services) is to be believed, then living in a strong nuclear family provides the best chance of getting a great education and successfully contributing to society through your career.

If the conclusions of the scholarly literature are correct then the data from Calgary should show such a correlation, and it generally does.

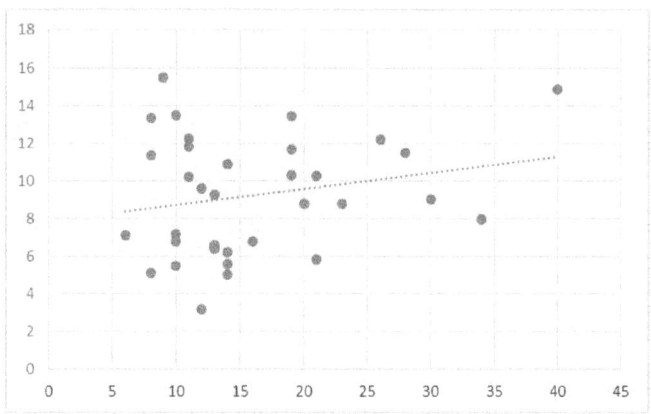

Figure 34 - Percent Common-Law vs Percent No High School

As the proportion of people without a high school education increases (further to the right on the horizontal axis) the percent of people in the community living in a common-law relationship slightly increases. Does that relationship hold for marriage?

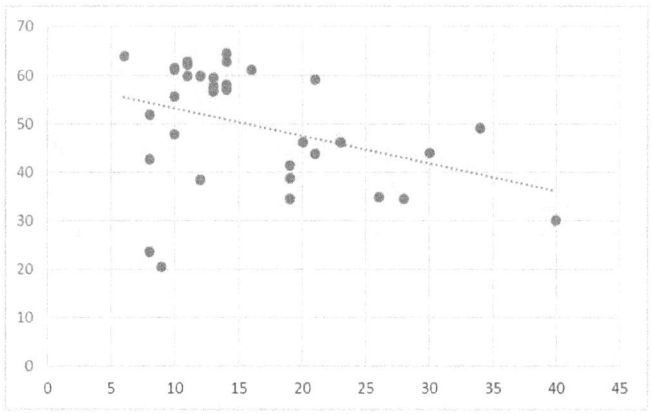

Figure 35 - Percent Married vs Percent No High School

In fact the reverse trend shows up. Communities with a larger proportion of people lacking a high school diploma also tend to have fewer married couples. In both cases, though, I think it is safe to say the correlation is on the weak side. The data is much more scattered and the trend is shallow. Similar results show up for unemployment; scatter with a weak correlation but still favouring marriage relationships over common-law.

But there is one indicator that showed a much strong correlation, and that is median income.

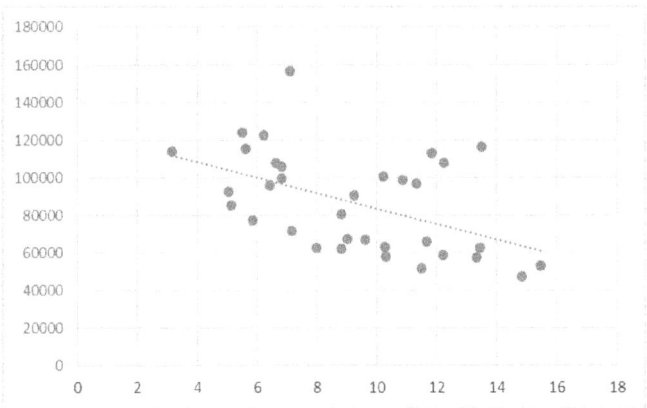

Figure 36 - Median Income vs Percent Common-Law

The data here is much clearer; communities with more common-law couples (further to the right on the horizontal axis) show a lower median income (vertical axis).

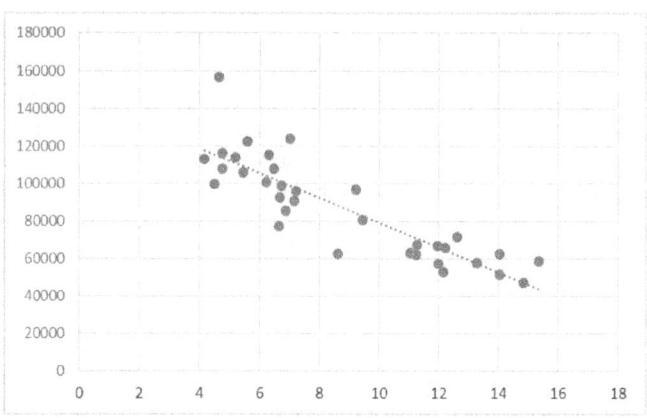

Figure 37 - Median Income vs Percent Separated / Divorced

Similar to common-law, the median income in the community is negatively correlated with the percent of people separated or divorced in that community.

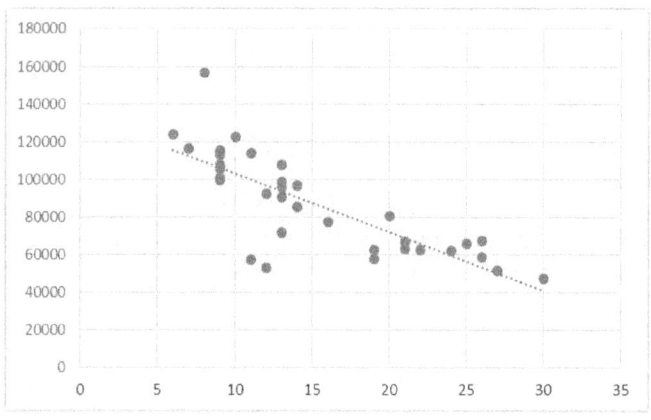

Figure 38 - Median Income vs Percent Lone Parents

And, not surprisingly, the median income in the community drops as the percent of lone parents increases. So those are many of the key alternatives to married families, so what about Marriage?

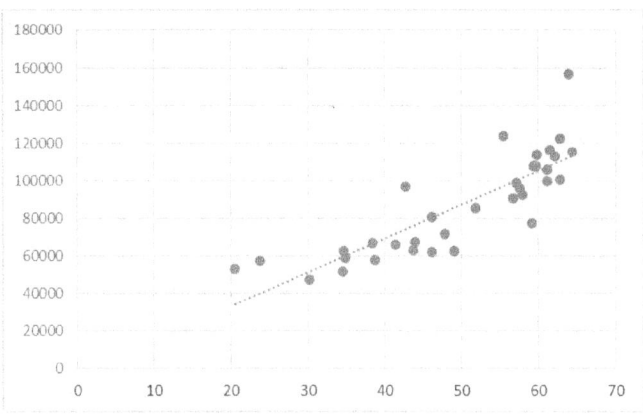

Figure 39 - Median Income vs Percent Married

This chart shows exactly the opposite correlation as all the others. As the percent of married couples in a community increases (further to the right on the horizontal axis) the median income also increases.

In summary, the trends described in the sociological research I listed are being lived out in the city of Calgary. Communities with a higher percent of people who choose family arrangements other than the gold standard are associated with a higher crime rate, lower median income, less education and more unemployment. If we can find ways of encouraging and empowering people to pursue the "gold standard" of married, biological parents raising their children in stable households, we will see an improvement in these measures. Traditional marriage is a key ingredient in a healthy society and the alternatives just don't measure up.

Commentary

The comments I made in the previous appendix about correlation not equaling causation apply here too. It is possible, for instance, that lack of education and lack of employment, and low income means people cannot afford to get married, so they live common-law instead. Their lack of sufficient means to live a reasonable lifestyle drives them to crimes like theft in order to make ends meet. Is that possible? Perhaps, but that's not the conclusion that the experts are coming to. As per the quotes I provided previously, sociologists are generally coming to the conclusion that it is the family break down that is leading to these other problems, not these other problems causing people to choose common-law arrangement when they would rather get married. If you don't like the interpretation then your beef is with sociologists of family, not with me.

These kinds of pro-family statements will inevitably come under attack. Despite the fact that it is sociologically fairly well established that the nuclear family is best for couples, kids and communities, people will offer all kinds of reasons to justify other arrangements, or at least why the government shouldn't give this family arrangement any preference over the alternatives. The biggest reason seems to be that not all kids in "non-nuclear" families end up in trouble; many grow up just fine. This is completely true, and nothing in what I've said suggests otherwise. The point about "statistically more likely" is that the results are not 100% guaranteed in all cases. Of course there are many exceptions; I can personally think of several in my own circle of friends and family.

But governments need to make policies based on the trends, not the exceptions. Not all sober drivers get home safe and sound, and not all drunk drivers end up killing people. But it is a well-established fact that drinking and driving is associated with a higher likelihood of serious risk. Based on this well-established trend (even though there are countless exceptions) the government implements policies that give preference to driving sober.

And, ironically, it may be the success stories from

common-law families that are more problematic than the failures. When a person considers buying a lottery ticket they do not think of the millions of people who lost money, they think only of the very small handful that won. They dream of being part of that elite crowd when they buy their ticket. Similarly, when a couple considers shacking up they don't think about all the common-law couples with very broken relationship histories and families, they are most likely to think of the success stories; the statistically few common-law couples that made it work.

This false sense of security inspires couples to "give it a shot" and thereby increases the number of families (and associated children) who will suffer as a result of the inevitable breakdowns from those many common-law families that do not enjoy the "happily ever after."

ABOUT THE AUTHOR

Paul is just an average Albertan. He does not have a degree in political science, economics or anything like that; he's only an engineer. He just thinks government should exist to help Albertans make this a great province without trying to do it for us through "helpful" but ultimately misguided progressive public policy.

www.ForTheLoveOfAlberta.com